Mamaila Nicholus

Village Poet Brighten the World

Mamaila Nicholus

Village Poet Brighten the World

Rural Poet makes the Sky to Limit... Consciousness Poetry to the People has brought Expertise and Life Awareness

JustFiction Edition

Imprint
Any brand names and product names mentioned in this book are subject to trademark, brand or patent protection and are trademarks or registered trademarks of their respective holders. The use of brand names, product names, common names, trade names, product descriptions etc. even without a particular marking in this work is in no way to be construed to mean that such names may be regarded as unrestricted in respect of trademark and brand protection legislation and could thus be used by anyone.

Cover image: www.ingimage.com

Publisher:
JustFiction! Edition
is a trademark of
International Book Market Service Ltd., member of OmniScriptum Publishing Group
17 Meldrum Street, Beau Bassin 71504, Mauritius

Printed at: see last page
ISBN: 978-620-0-48884-8

LET POOR PERSON SURVIVE

"You came poor and you will die poor"
"You precipitated to this planet and thou wilt evaporate the day you die"
"Opulent people are frolicking as how they match"…
"Nxaaa….Island yourself from us"
"Desert before season change"

All these utterances said my pals
Let me poor person survive
You loathed me is enough and
My poverty you sprinkled
My degree of lunatic you expanded
Let poor person survive

My body you dilated like elephant
My life you dehumanized
How deleterious are you?
Please, let me poor person survive

Forbears why are you sleeping, battle for me
My buddies are milking me like a cattle but I'm not
Boa constrictor under the grass makes unknown sound
Where will I run? Forebears bear me in mind
Let me poor person survive.
It is a long lane that has no turning,
All people I live with are expectorating me, why?
Let me poor person survive.

By Mamaila Nicholus

VOCABULARY USED FROM A POEM

Opulent people-Rich people
Frolicking-living together or playing together
Pals-friends you live with often
Loathed-hated or disliked
Sprinkled-irrigated or exaggerated
Degree of lunatic-amount of craziness
Dilated-body became bigger and wider
Dehumanized-not feeling and behaving like normal person
Deleterious-harmful and dangerous
Expectorating-to spit
Ol-all
Boa constrictor-an enemy (an American snake that is dangerous and moving underneath)

TERRITORY WILL BE MINE AGAIN

Africa my motherland Africa my place
The blue nature in Africa the nature that mesmerize outdoor riders
Comeback Africa comeback my motherland
Forever you are mine that is why I say territory will be mine again
They exploited you and their nails are polished as I say now
They took gold and diamond from Africa
They took all animals and lands I don't speak
They exploited the native Africans who endured in this womb
Please Africa comeback to your original people
Africa my needs provider and Africa my nurse that nurture my life
Africa my site of joy and place of emancipation
Aowa 27 years in jail is not a number to play lotto bravely I am *patriotic*
Africa recognizes her people and now are living in harmony
Territory will be mine again

Author: Mamaila Nicholus

VOCABULARY FROM A POEM

Mesmerize=to interest
Exploited=used for no payments
Native African=Original backs
Nurture=take care, to give foods and all things or to support
Site=a place
Siyabonga=a Zulu word that means "thank you"

OUR LOVELY COW'BREATH LEFT A CRY

We will recall you for your sense of humor
Friendliness and your affection
We don't interrogate gods' choice
But we feel you should have perished after there should have time to say a word.
Our lovely cow's breath left a cry

You left us with dung that we don't know belongs to
You left us silent and took our voice like an eagle taking a chick
All our yesterday has lightened us fools the way to dusty death
Your demise became our everyday shadow
We don't enjoy milk anymore because our lovely cow has passed away

Where will we hear those jokes once more?
Who will share them with us? Only good memories will abide.
We appreciate the good chance we had amalgamated
Like a bee to a flower hector, like a flower that has just opened its corolla
Our lovely cow's breath left a cry

Who will be our aunty in the future?
Who will rope us like a dog not to be lost?
Because life of these days is fast like tornado
We all pray god to prepare thy apartment in shalom and
You depicted us what life is and we won't forget
Eish.... Our lovely cow's breath left a cry

Author: By Mamaila Nicholus

VOCABULARY FROM A POEM

Interrogate=to Question
Abide=remain
Amalgamated=together
Perished =died
Recall=remember, to re-think

A ROAD BECAME MY NIGHTMARE

It was in the dead of night
En route to home
A white woman was aside awaiting to give birth or to rest I don't know
Sounds cry of death but help was not there
Her clothes were wet with water from the moon
And her hands were full of sin
Her heart was full of hatred
A road became my nightmare

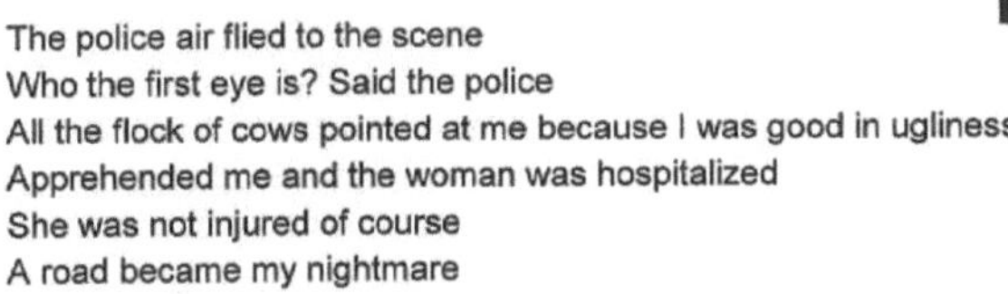

I called people to come and help
They appeared like a flock of cows coming to help
But they were afraid to help
An innocent child was dead as a doornail
A road became my nightmare

The police air flied to the scene
Who the first eye is? Said the police
All the flock of cows pointed at me because I was good in ugliness
Apprehended me and the woman was hospitalized
She was not injured of course
A road became my nightmare

Favourism in our motherland was depending on who you are
My life became futureless in jail
Jail became my death place because of being a first eye
Do not ever be a witness
Because it will turn your life to dark place
Jaaa…! Truly a road became my nightmare

Author: By Mamaila Nicholus

VOCABULARY FROM A POEM

Air-fly= to move by flying machine on air
Scene=place where events take place
Apprehended=to be jailed
En route= on a way to destination
Solo=alone
Dead as a doornail=completely dead

ALWAYS KEEP HER WORDS ON AIR

She proposes wages and roses
Vacant promises which sound like drums
I persisted dancing to her not stop chants for long
I think of the period not the wine
All I wanted was for me to be fine
I will draw the truth between the line of longitude and latitude
My current preparation cannot reach the recent generation because of promises
Promises all the time
She promised me love and I deserve more than promises
She never did anything to me but promises are the best
She was harmonious and melodic to me
My life is full of traumas
I am full of affection and she is full of promises and traumatic experiments
Is this torture or future?
Oooh.... no.... this is just promises and several promises

Author: By Mamaila Nicholus

VOCABULARY USED FROM POEM

Vacant-empty
Pledges-promises
Yearn-to wants something
Affection-truelove,
Traumas-pain of life experience, injuries
Current-right now, at this moment
Persisted-continued with determination

BLANKETS ARE COMMERCIAL TRADES

We never knew that bio wilt transmute
We never knew that life will be invisible to the naked eye
We never knew that we will have a pain of our loved one
But we did know that a smile of the cemetery will ride them to everlasting place
Blankets are commercial trades

We never knew that blankets will rain maladies
We never knew that toddles will have infants before parents
Is this emancipation we battled for?
We never knew of course that rights will impose sex
commercial trade
We never knew that sex trade will vomit orphans
Blankets are commercial trade

African juveniles dig their demise whilst are still alive
They perish immaturely and grow interior of their grave
Tire road dust whirlwind to our youths, they ate meat with no tooth
Recently suffering to wipe oil from their mouth
We never knew, let's embrace because is how life has revolutionized
Ooh blankets are commercial trade

Author: By Mamaila Nicholus

VOCABULARY USED FROM POEM

Transmute-change completely
Emancipation-liberty and freedom
Demise-a death
Immaturely-not matured and fully grown
Embrace-accept

BLESSED PILLOW MADE MY NIGHT

In my dreams, I saw an angel
Flying higher in the sky and trying so hard to reach her hands
I endeavored and wept aloud "take me my angel" ....
She scrutinizes at me with an elegant smile
At the end when I thoughts my dreams and ambitions are shattered
She came to my rescue like an autocue…smile…blessed pillow made my night
Wearing a white garment, she appeared a true angel looking so profound
More that gorgeous and put her signature across my heart
I cried; help me in shaping my fondness without shaking my spirits
Why she provokes my feelings? Especially moon lights
I provided myself to my angel, blessed pillow made my night
Believe it or not, you have changed my "phobia" and tears into cheers
At last I held and deserved love from my angel
Blessed pillow made my night

Author: By Mamaila Nicholus

VOCABULARY USED FROM THE POEM

Endeavor-try so hard to do something
Scrutinize-examined and analyzed carefully
Elegant-precious
Profound-very great
Gorgeous-more than handsome, highly beautiful
Phobia-very strong feelings of disliking
Shattered-destroyed and damaged seriously

HER RED LIGHTS WARNED HER

Her beauty turned her to silent place
Only the rainbow birds make the different songs and
Her spirits make trees to be strippers and grass to dance
On her grave ghost holds a bottle of wine and dancing from nature
 Insane ghost was thinking of a beauty of human a being not the wine
Ghost's alcoholic tears rolled down feeling it may be pardonable emphasizing that
"To err is human" but it was late for her Yrrrrr…her red lights warned her
She was warned to limit her ride her beauty was riding her ludicrously
She was still spinach that wanted to grow but sun burnt it
She was a saloon lamp that brighten ugly duckling brigand and dullard
She knew all kinds of wines and trouser pistols on her half age
She was red-light district and hussy girl for hustling
That's why her beauty turned her to a grave
Ja her red light warned her…a ghost's rhythm made a lesson to you and me

Author: Mamaila Nicholus

<u>VOCABULARY FROM A POEM</u>

Strippers=an entertainer who performs stripteases.
Pardonable=forgivable
Ludicrously=absurdly or extremely silly.
Spinach that wanted to grow=a young girl who still fresh and want to grow further.
Saloon=a bar or a place where people get drinks.
Brigand=bandit or a person who steel from travellers.
Dullard=someone who is not intelligent, or who does have thinking capacity.
Trouser pistol=a man's private organ he uses to have sex.
Red-lights district=an area with many prostitutes
Hussy girl=person who likes to attract men.
Hustling=selling sex to get money or to get something dishonestly

IF ONLY I HAD ALL EARS

If only I had all ears
Life was going to be sweat to live
I was going to drink honeycomb by fork
Unfortunately I defied getting consciousness
Informal educations were not my custom as parents were not given all ears
If only I had all ears

I was taking them as passerby like an insects flying to excrement.
Teachers admonished and sermonized until they become dumb
I was ineducable as hard as nail
Inebriation was an ineluctable pre I enter my lessons, how kitten was I?
If only I had all ears to the guidance of elders
If only life has a reverse, I was going to back my parents
If only I had all ears

I loose one's bearing in this life
I lay in the bed I have made
I'm now facing adult life solo
One quoth "ruthang bana di taola "…. oh no I bear in mind
Coz to me was not like that
Can I exhume my parents to proffer lesson?
Ooh Noo…! Only If I had all ears

During their demise, said I will follow the birds
I now suffer the evils I caused myself
"Who sleeps with dogs get up with fleas" said my teacher
If only I had all ears to listen,
Yooh….Is too late to make rectification
If only I had all ears

Author: By Mamaila Nicholus

<u>VOCABULARY USED FROM POEM</u>

Consciousness-Awareness
Excrement-solid waste that your body gets rid of
Admonished-advise someone not to do or do something
Sermonized-told to behave in a morally and correct way
Ineducable-unable to be taught or to be educated
Inebriation-Drunkenness
Ineluctable-impossible to avoid
Quoth-an old meaning 'Said"
Solo-alone
Proffer-to offer
Defied-disobeyed
Informal education-lesson you get from your parents like respect and culture

IS NEVER TOO LATE TO CHANGE

Is never too late to change
I deposited myself to notoriety
My feelings were deposit slip
My ID no was my account number in any bank branch
My mind became notorious branch
My legs drove me absurdly and lethally
But is never too late to deviate
I currently yearn to withdraw myself from the predicament I am

My eyes are burning conflagrations
The mouth is uttering the smoke
Is true that.....curiosity killed the cat
But is never too late to derive out of this notorious life
Chicken's regime was my authority
Yes....is never too late to change
Long way does not mean that we can give up

Still the race can be yours
Hard life was my middle name and bur glaring was my daily bread
Money I took unblinkingly
Mendacity I used to survive
I now lament and expressing a sorrowful cry
Yes.... is never too late to change

Author: By Mamaila Nicholus

<u>VOCABULARY USED FROM A POEM</u>

Notoriety=situation where you are famous of bad things
Predicament=a situation that is unpleasant or bad
Unblinkingly=look something for a long time without closing eyes
Mendacity=lie
Conflagrations=fire

MONEY MAKETH MARE TO GO

Money maketh mare to go
Money endangers our lives like a pre-born baby,
Scorched by a cup of a tea
The world is full of lies these days
Parliaments are doing things in a fraudulent path because of money
Money maketh mare to go………

Money opens our ways and at the end places us in jail
Juveniles I see no future, why?
Because love coercion is manipulating them
Life transformed a tornado because of money
Money maketh mare to go

Idolatry controls our lives like papers moving up by whirlwind
Money makes a wife to patronize her husband
People are lacking to consume, to dress, to survive because of money
Money maketh mare to go

Why egoli the site of money helps our people?
Why don't you conceive money and throw to your people?
Like a capacious rain filling the oceans
 One said money makes the mares to go
The mares will arrive where they are going
Money maketh mare to go

Author: By Mamaila Nicholus

VOCABULARY FROM A PEOM

Mare=an adult female horse.
Juveniles=the youths.
Love Coercion=love involving threats or property, money.
Manipulating=to influencing someone o control in a clever and dishonest way
Idolatry=the worship of idol or something admired very much.
Patronize=to behave in a way that you think you are better than others
Egoli=a Zulu word that means Gauteng
Capacious=huge, big or profound

MOTHER OF WARM HANDS

The warm hands I did not see
Yep… the time I was an infant like an ant
I was blind and untouchable child like a plastic filled with water
But a good mother elevated me in mercy
I recently see and gallivanting around
Her breast was an ocean to remove thirst
Mother of warm hands

Her pikapoos were hourly entertainment to see my canine
She was bouncing me like a butterfly that flies to a corolla of flower
But I was nervous and crying like a chicken in the morning
Soft porridge was my daily food as I was toothless, I used to drink it
The warm hands had consistency to raise my life
True mother knows her kitten
Hmmmm…. mother of warm hands

You are above the board to me
The love I did never see from thou
Your love is an ocean; it does not embrace dirty to her child
Thanks for 2day and tomorrow…
Oooh… Yes yesterday you have been planning to be with me
True mother I did not see
Mother of warm hands

Author: By Mamaila Nicholus

<u>VOCABULARY FROM A POEM</u>

Infant=a small child
Elevated=raised
Gallivant=to go from place to place
Mercy=with peace
Kitten=a young cat
Embrace=to accept

Contextual Questions: Let the poor person survive.

1) Who is the author and give one meaning of the word *author*?
2) To whom you think the poet was referring when he says "let the poor person survive"?
3) What tone expressed by stanza 1?
4) What is the motive/purpose for writing this poem?
5) "Desert before season change" in your own understanding what does it mean and what type of speech deployed on the word 'desert'?
6) Which word appears and suggests that a poet is not feeling and behaving like a normal person?
7) Where and how many times the title appears in the poem and what is the effect of repetition?
8) What is Boa Constrictor line 18?

Contextual Question: Territory will be mine again

1) Why the Title of this poem says "Territory will be mine again, not saying Territory will be mine"?

2) Identify the form of this poem and portray the structure.

3) Why does poet spell Africa with a capital letter?

4) Who took animals and lands from Africa according to the poem?

5) When do you think this poem set? Explain your option.

6) What is a sonnet?

7) According to your understanding of apartheid, why do you think Africa snatched from Native African?

8) Give a simple meaning of the phrase "Native African" line 8

9) Explain ,why do you think a poet says Africa my motherland

10) Who do you think was reciting Africa?

11) Choose which of the following figure of speech poet used line 13 to make poem memorable:
   a) Simile

   b) Irony

   c) Personification

12) Africa is a continent with prosperity. Support your answer

13) Define the term "Territory"

14) Poet became thrilled and wise to use the phrase "Outdoor Riders" explain the point that a poet is trying to communicate with the readers?

15) Which of the following describe the poet's tone suitably?

   a) Aggressive and Bitter

   b) Abrasive

   c) Amicable

16) What does the poet mean of following sentence and to whom is he referring? Line5

   a) "Their nails are polished"

17) Explain the word exploitation in your own understanding.

Contextual Question: Our lovely cow's breath left a cry

1) Explain the figure of speech used on the heading.
2) What type of poem is this?
3) What is the tone of this poem?
4) Portray, what poet import when says "our lovely cow's breath left a cry"
5) Give a **synonym** of the word "demise" in line 9?
6) What do you think was the poet's purpose in writing this poem?
7) In stanza 4, a poet utilized simile. Substantiate your answer by quoting seven consecutive words
8) Explain, the emotional dimensions or the emotional characteristics of the person represented in the poem.
9) Why a poet used repetition of "our lovely cow's breath left a cry" to any stanza?
10) Describe the moods and emotions of the poet on the last sentence.
11) Explain line 3 using your own words
12) Punctuate the Title with the relevant punctuation mark.

Contextual Question: A Road Became My Nightmare

1. Which of the following words would you use to describe poet when scrutinizing the heading?
   a) Afraid
   b) Dreaming
   c) Scared
   d) Angry

   i) A and B
   ii) B and C
   iii) A and C
   iv) C and D

2. At what time a road became nightmare to him and where was he going to?
3. Why do you think white woman was waiting aside the road and what was the sound line 3 & 4?
4. Which full sentence shows that child was completely dead and what is it that poet used to spice the sentence?
5. Consult bible to quote a verse against murder.
6. Why poet says her hands were full of sin?
7. Explain, how did the cops arrive to the scene?
8. Why did police arrest the poet than to arrest white woman who killed an innocent blood?
9. Stanza 3 smell sour flavour of inequality, comment on a country with no gender equality.
10. What lesson you learn from last stanza?
11. On which sestet did poet use third person?

Contextual Question: Always keep her words on air

1) A poet obscured simple meaning of the title. Explain in a simple way
2) Which word showing that she demands money from poet?
3) Why do you think a poet do not stop song, he keeps on dancing with her?
4) What are the vacant promises?
5) Give one word (**synonyms**) to the following
    a) Yearn
    b) Persisted
    c) Recent
    d) Wages
    e) Roses
    f) Chants
6) Poet demonstrated that his life is full with traumas, how can this happen according to the poet?
7) Be analytic and think deeply to this poem and find out what illness poet hath?
8) Explain the word harmonious and melodic.

Contextual Question: Blankets are commercial trades

1) Comment on the usage of the word **"We"**?
2) Give synonym of the sentence "Bio wilt transmute"
3) Summarize the title in 2 to 3 sentences.
4) How many stanzas are used?
5) What do they cause when selling their body?
6) To whom a poet is asking in line 8?
7) Poet says "toddles will have infants before parents" and that is impossible, what does he try to say?
8) Do you think tolerating the "rights" strayed many children?
9) "Sex trade will vomit orphans" how?
10) Comment on frequent use of repetition in the structure of the poem. Why do you think it suits the topic?
11) What figure of speech used line 13 "they perished immaturely and grow interior of their grave"
    a) Litotes
    b) Hyperbole
    c) Irony
12) The word "They" refers to whom in line 13?

Contextual Question: Blessed pillow made my night

1) Explain purpose or possible motives for writing the poem
2) What is a tone?
3) The word "**SHE**" represents who according to this poem?
4) What are the personal feelings does poet reveal?
5) Simile is a figure of speech in which both things essentially differ but thought to be alike in certain characteristics, True or False? Support your answer with quotes.
6) Explain how poet changes his tone in line 3 and line 12.
7) A poet is dreaming daylights. True or False? Quote three consecutive words to support your answer.
8) Comment on the use of the term *"Phobia"*

Contextual Question: Her red lights warned her

1) Use your own words to explain the Title
2) What kind of a poem is this?
3) Who has warned by her red lights?
4) What is the central theme of the poem?
5) Where do you think rainbow birds make the different songs line 2?
6) Account for the use of pronoun from line 8-12?
7) Which figure of speech took place in line 3?
8) Differentiate between the types of speech and figures of speech
9) Poet denoted that "She" was weeping. Prove it by quoting three words.
10) What massage does the poem convey?
11) How does poet describe "She" according to your understanding?

Contextual Question: Only if I had all ears

1) **Choose** True or False

   a) To have all ears means to pay much attention and listen what you are told

2) What feelings or emotions expressed by the words "If only I had all ears?

3) Comment on the use of "If" within the context.

4) What are the formal educations stanza 1?

5) Why does he use the word "I" so often?

6) Comment on line 14 and 15

7) Which one word shows that a poet is drinking alcohol?

8) Quote the phrase proofing that a poet wished to live better life and explain the meaning using your own words

9) Explain, poet compare his parents with what? And what figure of speech is that?

10) Who became mute when trying to advice a poet?

11) Quote a sentence showing that a poet has influenced by his friends and explain or comment on it?

12) The word **"Yooh"** conveys the message or action. Explain

13) Why he opened his poem with "if only I had all ears and also once again end up with "if only I had all ears"?

Contextual Question: Is never too late to change

1) Why a poet emphasizes "is never too late to change"?
2) What is the purpose and target group of this poem?
3) Explain the poet's phrase of choice "My legs drove me absurdly and lethally"
4) Poet said "my mind became notorious branch" what does it mean?
5) Quote 1 line in stanza 2 that shows certainly a poet wants to change from life he opted.
6) Try to work out a possible meaning for "uttering the smoke" line 10.
7) Figure of speech is used line 11, explain the meaning and why do you think is suitable to this poem?
8) A poet is a rapist. Motivate and prove your answer with quoting six consecutive words.
9) To show understanding of poetry language, define the word "consecutive" and re-write into adverb.
10) **Choose True or False**
    a) Mendacity means rumours
    b) Unblinkingly means glaring without closing eye-lash
11) What lessons and external motivations do we get in general from the poem?

Contextual question: Money Maketh Mare to go

1) Explain the alliteration
2) What is an alliteration
3) Poet used proverb by this title "money maketh mare to go". Explain its meaning
4) What are quatrains and where are utilized within the paragraph?
5) To whom a poet is referring when he says 'why don't you conceive money and throw to your people. Why?
6) Give other word for "Egoli"
7) What is love coercion line 9?
8) "Life transformed tornado" comment on the phrase
9) Explain what a poet means "Idolatry controls our lives like papers moving up by whirlwind"

Contextual Question: Mother of Warm Hands.

1) Why a poet opens his poem by the word 'warm hands I did not see?

2) Poet recite mother of warm hands, why?

3) Use adjectives to describe the mother of warm hands he speaks off.

4) Poet used funniest sentences in line 2 and line 3, but it seems making sense and logic, comment on it.

5) How old do you estimate a poet was? Quote four words to substantiate your respond.

6) What was the plan of poet's mother when she wanted to see front teeth?

7) Why a poet compares a breast with an ocean?

8) Two adjective on the context can suggest that a poet was born as a pre-mature when he was born. Quote

9) Give your conceptions to this *"hmmmm"* stanza 2.

10) Give one word to this phrase "you are above the board"

11) Re-write the word *2day* in a formal way and why do you think a poet wrote it like this?

Answers to the Poem: Let poor person survive

English First Additional Language

1) Mamaila Nicholus✓ Author means Writer✓
2) To his friends/ to his enemies✓

3) Tone of hatred✓

4) A poet wants to inform and aware his enemies to leave him in peace✓

   To notify his friends that he heard enough by their bad or negative treatment✓

   Publicise bad treatment from bad friends✓ **Choose one**

5) It commands a poet that must leave from his enemies because they can change their mind to think negatively to take his life.✓ He used the word "Desert" as a **Verb**.✓

6) Dehumanized✓

7) Repetitions occur from stanza 2 and 3, ✓it appears 5 times to the entire poem. ✓The repetition makes the readers not to haunts or to stay disturbingly in the mind and also grasp the poet's purpose or main thoughts.✓

8) Boa constrictor is a strong American serpent but a poet used the word as an enemy to this poem

Answers to the poem: Territory will be mine again

English First Additional Language

1) It shows that territory was belonging to the poet before.✓
2) It is a sonnet, it has 14 lines ✓and it has a regular rhyme, ✓it has formed without punctuation mark.✓
3) He gives the idea of Africa a name, because names of continents and countries are always written in capital.✓
4) The whites/people from England.✓
5) In 1990, because Nelson Mandela was arrested in 1963 and he lived in jail for two decades plus 7 years.✓✓
6) Form of poetry where the poem has 14 lines and has regular rhythm.✓
7) The blacks were uneducated and the whites came with technology to blind Africans.✓
8) Native African are the indigenous or original citizen, the founder of Africa, the "**khoikhois**" are the native Africans
9) It indicates that a poet was born in Africa and he fights for it✓
10) Nelson Rolihlahla Mandela✓
11) C) Personification✓
12) 'Gold and Diamond from Africa'✓
13) Territory= is the area ✓or the land that belongs to the original Africans✓
14) People from overseas visit to Africa.✓
15) Aggressive and Bitter.✓ or A✓
16) He refers the whites, they are rich and successful, they have everything and they own money in Africa.✓
17) Treating someone as a slave, unfairly and using him hard work to benefits from his resources

Answers to the poem: Our lovely cow's breath left a cry

English First Additional language

1) Personification.✓
2) Elegy. Because is reciting a person who has died and it sounds great sadness and pains for losing the beloved one.✓
3) It sounds with unhappiness, painful and sad tone✓
4) Poet tries to indicate that the beloved one has left him with a great pain he never had and tears rolled across his cheeks (cried) when losing his family member.✓He means that the beloved family member was a bread winner because she has died; she left them with poverty and crises.✓
5) Death✓
6) The purpose was to remember and show the last respect to their lovely aunt who cared for while alive. ✓Was to dignify the integrity and show love to the deceased for the last chance.✓Was to say the last good words for good and to pay a humble respect.
7) "like a dog not to be lost"✓
8) She had sense of humour, she had love, care, she had true generosity, kindness and she was approachable and open✓
9) Poet tries to be poetic and he expresses the feeling of pain that comes persistently from his mind✓
10) It express painful feelings✓
11) We appreciate everything made by a will of God ✓
12) Apostrophe '✓ / Our lovely cow's breath left a cry✓ **Choose One**

47

Answers to the Poem: Road became my nightmare
English First Additional Language

1) **Choose Multiple Choice**

   iii) A and C

2) It was in the middle of the night/the dead of the nights/ **00h00**.✓ Any relevant answer
   He was on his way to home/ en route to home✓

3) White woman was on pain labor, she was nine months pregnant ✓and she birthed aside the road and she after kill an infant✓.

4) "an innocent child was dead as a doornail"✓Poet used an idiom ✓

5) Exodus chapter 20 verse 13 says "you must not murder"✓

6) Because she has killed an innocent blood/ she committed murder.

7) Arrived with flight/ fly machine/ helicopter ✓**Choose One**

8) Because of favour, racial segregation and he also arrested to be first witness of the incidents.✓

9) Country with no Gender Equality is more likely to have higher domestic violence rates✓

10) It teaches people to know that witnessing suppose not or must not be their first best choice✓ because we end up being the suspect of the incidents and loss whatever we hoped to achieve, we also become the jail birds in the behind bars.✓

11) Third stanza✓ / 3rd Stanza ✓/ Poet used "SHE" as third person on stanza 3.✓ **Choose One**

49

Answers to the Poem: Always keep her words on air
English First Additional Language

1) A poet means that she does not fulfil her promises, she fails to achieve the spoken words✓
2) Wages✓
3) Poet still awaiting a reply from her because if he let her go, she will never come back with feedback.✓✓
4) The promises that do not happen, the empty promises.✓
5) Synonyms
    i.   Want✓
    ii. Continued✓
    iii. Now✓
    iv. Salaries✓
    v.   Flowers✓
    vi. Song✓
6) A poet is traumatized emotionally and mentally because he keeps on thinking and waiting empty promises, he is financially demanded and he does not get something that pleases him in return✓✓
7) Lovesick✓
8) "Harmonious and melodic are adjective, ✓ are used correctly on the sentence, peacefully and friendly ✓

29

Answers to the Poem: Blankets are commercial trade
English First Additional Language

1) A poet used pronoun of "We" to generalize and to omit the name of particular person. ✓
2) Life will change ✓
3) Youths are selling their body to generate money and they take sex as an everyday business because they want to push life to better survive, sex is a business to our people especially current generation. ✓
4) Three stanzas. ✓ **or** 3th stanzas ✓
5) Sexual Transmitted Disease ✓ Disease or Maladies ✓ **Choose One**
6) Is asking the liberated country, the government and or the parents, leaders and whoever who is a victim of sex trade, it covers all the citizens, freedom fighters and others in the nation ✓ ✓
7) Children are intended and apt to know many things when they are not supposed to know than their parents. Poet used hyperbole to exaggerate the statement. ✓
8) **Yes.** Because they misuse the rights and they die before time ✓
   They no longer giving attention to the elderly people and they disregard ✓
9) People do unprotected sex and get affected by STIs, when they die, children become parentless ✓
10) This poem represents announcement /notice to the people as most are not familiar with ✓ aftermath of trading body, poet repeat information to eye open the body trader ✓
11) B/ Hyperbole ✓
12) Refer Sex Trader ✓ Youths ✓

Answers to the Poem: Blessed pillow made my night
English First Additional Language

1) He wrote the poem to praise and to tell the **girl** how he feels, how the dreams were and he also wants to absorb the interests and take her home in loving him(to convince)✓
   He wrote the poem to be loved by the girl on his dreams✓
2) Tone is a feeling of words, the words have to tell the readers what expression is within the poem✓
3) She represents the poet's Girl Friend on his dream✓
4) Feelings of great love/ joy to happiness✓
5) True. "she came to my rescue like an autocue"✓
6) In line three poet is crying and tears roll down but at the end of the poem in line 12✓ everything changed to happiness, Is cheerful because he loved by his angel.✓
   ✓   ✓
7) **False.** "especially moon lights" the moon only appears at night
8) Instead of using the word hatred, a poet used the suffix of *"phobia"* ✓

33

Answers to the Poem: Her red lights warned her

English First Additional Language

1) Parents always guide a child✓
2) Is a sonnet, it has 14 lines✓
3) Young girl/youth✓
4) Explain the effects of ignorance✓
5) At the cemetery✓
   A place where corps are buried✓
6) **"She"** remove all individuality as a person is known by name✓
7) Personification✓
8) **Types of speech** are the auxiliary words that create a particular language in the use of Verbs, Nouns, adverbs, adjectives and pronouns. The Figure of speech is when a poet use or creates a sentence figuratively than making it literally.
9) Tears rolled down✓
10) It guides that ignorance is dangerous and show off does not contribute positively to our lives. It also advice that respecting the words of parents will put us to everlasting life.
11) He describes her as a bitch girl, ✓as someone who is ignorant and street rider. She is a person who interested to nice time and absent her minds to the consequences. A girl who was young but abandoned her life while alive. ✓

Answers to the Poem: If only I had all ears
English First Additional Language

1) True✓
2) The words express sorrow and regrets✓
3) He knows that his life is in danger by not listening and he thinks that, what if he should have listened perchance he should have not being in the present situation✓
4) The lessons and respect you taught by elderly people, culture, manners and other education you get at home while growing✓
5) He is individual. He tries to omit his name by using pronoun of "I"✓
6) A poet used idioms to catch the eyes of the readers. ✓To get lost (confused) and suffer the results of one's deeds✓
7) Inebriation✓
8) "I was going to drink honeycomb by fork"✓poet used metaphor to emphasize that he was going to live good and large, have everything, all the wants and the needs, was going to have pride of what he has. ✓ **Any relevant answer**
9) As passerby like insects fly to excrement✓
   He used simile to compare✓
10) "Teachers adnormished and sermonized until they become dumb"✓
   He used metaphor; he means that they spoke until they give up✓
11) "Who sleeps with dog get up with fleas"✓
   Is a proverb, it means evil friends have a bad influence on one's character✓
12) A poet is crying and lamenting✓
13) He is trying to emphasize that to listen is important and regretting is an impediments ✓
   He expresses his feelings from the start to an end✓
   He is poetic and wants to make it unforgettable✓

37

Answers to the poem: Is never too late to change

English First Additional language

1) Poet does not want to lose hope, he keeps on motivating and encouraging himself with using the words frequently✓✓

2) The purpose is to divulge his lifestyle and report himself with apology to the victims he hurt before, he needs forgiveness from people he tortured. He wants people to know him as a new person than before, he wants to create new life with people in harmony. ✓ ✓

3) He means that the route he chose was moving him silly, ludicrously and his legs were dead, he never knew where he moves, he used a figure of speech (metaphor) to make up the sentence ✓✓

4) He is corrupt, everything he thinks to do, has bad effects and is known of bad things✓

5) "I currently yearn to withdraw myself from the predicament".✓

6) Telling lies to the people✓

7)

8) Chicken's regime was my authority.✓

9) Consecutive means the words or things that are following each other or series of things orderly.✓ **Adverb** "Consecutively" ✓

10) A False.✓

   B True✓

11) It plants good advices and informs the target group of gangsters that bad attitudes put a person to bad altitudes.✓✓

Answers to the Poem: Money Maketh Mare to go
English First Additional Language

1) Money Maketh Mare✓
2) Is the repetition of similar consonant sounds✓
3) One can do most things if one has the money✓
4) Quatrain is a four-line stanza , poet used quatrain in stanza 3✓
5) He refers to **"egoli"** (Gauteng) because is where money generated and where gold generated. ✓
   He used personification to personify egoli with a female person because female person or a mother is always loving and ✓caring, that's why he compares egoli with a mother person.✓
6) Gauteng✓
7) Love coercion is the love which involving property , money and or fancy things, loving because of status and advantages✓the love relationship looking the benefits ✓
8) This is figure of speech contains deliberate and simple exaggeration, is not meant to be taken literally poet used hyperbole and diction.✓
9) Poet compares people with papers because they do not have constant direction; they worship money as their idols. ✓

Answers to the poem: Mother of warm hands
English First Additional language

1) Poet tries to catch readers' mind to admire the mother's unlimited love, ✓nothing important than having a mother who cares✓
2) He feels proud of how mother of warm hands raised him and that indicates appreciations to his mother✓
3) She is loving, caring and consistent ✓
4) Poet used simile to compare himself with an ant, when he was infant, he did not see how the love of his mother was. ✓
5) Three days old. "blind and untouchable"✓
6) She does pikapoo games and she entertain him to laugh✓
7) Ocean hath everything that people needs to survive, ✓ the same applies to the breast of his mother if it was not because of breast a poet should have died✓
8) Blind and untouchable✓
9) That express the feelings of the poet that he enjoys to grow, he is satisfied with the love he got from his loving mother and he feels happy to be himself.✓
10) Honest, Reliable, trustable, believable✓ **Choose One**
11) Today. Poet is avoiding to use more letters within one word

45

I want morebooks!

Buy your books fast and straightforward online - at one of world's fastest growing online book stores! Environmentally sound due to Print-on-Demand technologies.

Buy your books online at
www.morebooks.shop

Kaufen Sie Ihre Bücher schnell und unkompliziert online – auf einer der am schnellsten wachsenden Buchhandelsplattformen weltweit! Dank Print-On-Demand umwelt- und ressourcenschonend produziert.

Bücher schneller online kaufen
www.morebooks.shop